You and the
Metric System

Allan C. Stover

You and the Metric System

Illustrated by Charles Jakubowski

DODD, MEAD & COMPANY · NEW YORK

To the hundreds of millions of Americans of future genera-tions who will live in a metric world and be free from today's measurement confusion.

ACKNOWLEDGMENTS

I am grateful to W. R. Tilley of the National Bureau of Standards for his help and insight into the U. S. Metric Study, which provided much of the background material for this book. I also wish to thank Ginny McDaniels, Ohio Department of Transportation; A. Bryan Marvin, Monsanto Company; the B. F. Goodrich Company; and numerous other individuals and corporations for their valuable help.

—A.C.S.

Contents

Contents

1

The Metric System
Is Coming

Someday, you will use only the metric system for measurements. You will buy coffee by the kilogram, milk by the liter, and land by the hectare. The ounce, pound, acre, foot, yard, inch, mile, pint, quart, gallon, bushel, and peck will fade away. These units will sound as strange to future generations as the pottle and wey do to you.

You probably know little about the metric system. Don't worry; you have company. According to a government study, only three out of twenty-five Americans know a great deal about it. Although the metric system will disrupt our lives, few of us have bothered to learn it.

The metric changeover will affect your home, career, and everyday life. The impact on schools, industry, government, and the military will be tremendous. If you learn the metric system, you will have a head start in school, in your career, at home, in the market, and on the road.

OUR FRIENDS OVERSEAS

When the United States switches to the metric system, she joins the rest of the world, except for a handful of small nations. At last count, only Burma, Barbados, Ghana, Liberia, Nauru, Oman, Sierra Leone, Southern Yemen, Tonga, and the United States have stood their ground against the metric onslaught.

All other nations use the metric system, or have committed themselves to a changeover. Even Great Britain, who gave us much of our present system (called the *customary* or *English* system), will soon be completely metric.

The rest of the world can't understand our measurement system; we can't understand theirs. We can't "think metric"; they can't "think customary." This causes massive problems in this day of satellite communications, jet travel, and international trade.

The time for this isolationism has passed. It makes as little sense for us to use a different measurement system as it does for you to use a different system from your neighbor. Suppose he decides to use the Biblical units, and you use the troy weight system. While he speaks of lengths in cubits and leagues, you speak of weights in grains and pennyweights. You can't understand each other.

8

Our neighbor, Mexico, is a metric nation. But she maintains a dual system—the metric for local use and the customary for dealing with us. Canada has committed herself to a change to metric, but she hesitates to change until we do. She fears that too many problems could arise in her dealing with us.

Our world would be more harmonious if all nations used a single system of measurement. We use a standard-size battery for our flashlights, a standard light bulb for a standard socket, and a standard nut for a standard bolt. This uniformity prevents chaos in our lives. Similarly, we should standardize our measurements with the rest of the world.

Our important customers overseas use the metric system. They do consider other factors in our products more important, such as reputation, price, and reliability, but our use of a different system of measurement does account for a decrease in exports. Four out of ten exporters agree that the metric changeover will boost our sales abroad. A government report says, "A potential customer in another country may prefer a certain U.S. machine, but he may be less likely to import it if parts for repair and maintenance are not readily available in his country."

When European cars, with their metric-sized bolts and nuts, first arrived in the United States in quantity, auto mechanics almost revolted. They disliked the metric parts. Some experienced difficulties because they lacked metric tools. Some opposed the cars for patriotic reasons. Others were confused by the metric units and refused to work on any foreign car. They tried to talk their customers out of buying foreign cars and "buy American" instead.

Americans finally accepted the foreign cars because they knew that metric imports were inevitable. But other nations can refuse American products with their customary-sized parts. Local products cost less, and foreign customers know that the customary system will soon go. Parts scaled to customary sizes will one day become difficult to obtain locally.

ENGINEERING STANDARDS

Of as much concern is the difference in engineering standards. Engineering standards set certain sizes or characteristics of things. They standardize anything that can be described or measured, such as the width of recording tape, the size of envelopes and paper, the contents of hot dogs, the frequency of a television channel, the strength of an automobile bumper, and thousands of others. A company sets standards for its products; a city government writes building codes; the U.S. government sets standards on products it buys from manufacturers. A standard is written by experts who set down what they consider the best way to do things.

Without standards, we would encounter confusion, shoddy products, and higher prices. Mass production is possible because two parts are standard sizes that fit together. Medicines that fail to meet standards could endanger our lives. An airplane must comply with hundreds of standards before it can be flown.

We base most of our engineering standards on customary units. Metric nations base theirs on the metric system. As a result, our standards differ from those of other countries.

Experts who write standards try to make them easy to understand and remember. They select sizes and quantities that are simple fractions or whole numbers. An industrial association in a metric country sets the diameter of one particular size of cable at exactly two centimeters (.7874 inches) because it is an even number. The same type of association in the United States would pick an even .8 inches as the ideal size. The two cables measure almost the same size, but they differ slightly.

A buyer in a metric nation would reject the .8 inch cable because it fails to meet local standards and differs from that sold locally. He purchases two-centimeter cable because his customers recognize the size.

Abroad, American industry still ranks first in areas where our technology has taken the lead, such as computers and electronic integrated circuits. But in many areas, we lost our lead years ago, especially where our products fail to meet *international standards*. International standards are engineering stan-

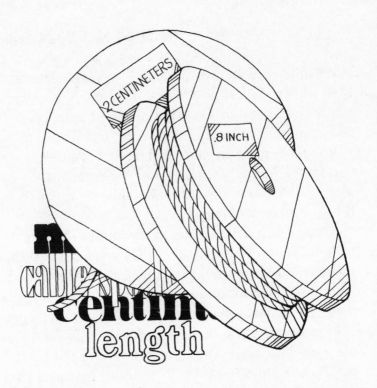

dards that are adopted by an international conference. The number of these standards has soared out of sight in the last few years. Where U.S. industry sets the standards, our products have a small edge over others. We sorely need this edge, as one look at our balance of payments will show.

EASE OF COMPUTATION

Another reason in support of a metric changeover is the ease of computations. Other systems lack the simplicity of the metric system.

The following table compares some common units of the metric system with our customary system. Notice that the customary system uses many different units to express the same quantity. Sometimes, it uses one unit for two different quantities. There is a fluid quart and a dry quart. The ounce is used for both weight and capacity. The metric system uses one unit for each quantity and is thus less confusing.

METRIC	CUSTOMARY
Length: meter	inch
	foot
	yard
	nautical mile
	statute mile
	rod
	fathom
	chain
	furlong
Mass: kilogram	ounce
	pound
	ton
	pennyweight
	dram
	hundredweight
	grain
	scruple

METRIC	CUSTOMARY
Capacity: liter	ounce (dry and liquid)
cubic meter	minim
	dram
	teaspoon
	tablespoon
	cup
	gill
	pint (dry and liquid)
	quart (dry and liquid)
	gallon (dry and liquid)
	peck
	bushel
	barrel

In the metric system, the meter is the basic unit of length. In the customary system, we can measure length in inches, feet, yards, or miles, among others. Capacity in the metric system is measured in liters or cubic meters. In the customary system, we can measure capacity in at least thirteen different units.

Customary units are related to each other by awkward conversion factors, most of which have neither rhyme nor reason. A yard contains 36 inches; a mile, 1760 yards; a pound, 16 ounces. Metric units are based on the decimal system, as is our money. The number of nations that have converted to a decimal system of coinage shows the wisdom of a decimal system. Multiples and fractions of metric units are related by even powers of ten.

To make matters worse, we mix customary units. We speak of a distance as 12 feet, 3 inches; a weight as 3 pounds, 6 ounces. Metric units are unmixed, and fractions are never expressed as a new unit. A metric length is expressed as 4.2 meters, never 4 meters, 20 centimeters.

SCHOOL DAYS

In education, the metric system will trigger a minor revolution, especially in the lower grades. Studies in Great Britain and Australia show that the metric changeover in their nations could save a fifth of the time previously spent teaching mathematics. A U.S. government report estimates the time saved in our schools could run from 15 to 25 per cent.

One of the nation's largest educational associations gave this view on the metric system: "The National Education Association believes that a carefully planned effort to convert to the metric system is essential to the future of American industrial and technological development and to the evolution of effective world communication." They urged all teachers to teach the metric system as the primary system of weights and measures in the United States.

A science teacher's association listed several advantages of a changeover to metric. Briefly, here are the main points:

—Since the metric system uses the base 10, it's easier

for students to understand and remember.

—Conversions and calculations are much easier.

—Mathematical tasks will interfere less with the teaching of science.

—Measurements are more precise.

They listed no disadvantages.

Children who are now in the elementary grades will celebrate their thirtieth birthday near the turn of the century. If our nation fails to prepare them to use the metric system, an entire generation will be handicapped.

OTHER SUPPORT

Six out of ten government agencies support a metric changeover and believe it will benefit the nation. The National Bureau of Standards, the agency responsible for America's weights and measures, adopted the metric system as far back as 1964. The National Aeronautics and Space Administration kicked off its conversion program a few years ago. The scientific influence was a key reason for NASA's decision to change over. Scientists and engineers have used the metric system for decades.

American industry also backs the changeover. Seven out of ten manufacturers and six out of ten nonmanufacturers say that the metric system will benefit the nation.

Labor unions support the changeover, though they

are wary of tool replacement costs and retraining for their members. They worry about "loss of experience." An aircraft mechanic with ten years experience automatically grabs the right wrench when he works on an engine. During the first few months he works on metric engines, his experience fails him. He wastes time searching for the correct wrench. This loss of experience has already caused problems and will worsen as more metric products appear on the market.

HERE IT COMES

The hardest part of the changeover to swallow are the costs. Most people overestimate them, and fail to consider future benefits and savings. Some costs are false; they would have been required anyway. The costs of replacing textbooks in the schools, for example, will run into billions of dollars. But schools change textbooks every five years or so anyway. If they wait until their textbooks wear out before replacing them with metric texts, they will experience no extra costs.

The costs of going metric will run less now than later. And no matter what happens, we will someday become a metric nation anyway. Experts at the National Bureau of Standards figure that the nation will drift toward a total changeover within fifty years—and this is the most expensive way to change.

About eighteen years ago, U.S. drug manufacturers converted to the metric system. They found their costs were lower than expected, as much as 50 per cent below estimates. They believe they have already recouped their losses and now enjoy the benefits of the metric system.

Another bitter pill to swallow is the change of "sacred measurements," such as the size of a football field or baseball diamond. These examples fall under the "rule of reason." If a changeover in any area will serve no useful purpose, the measurements may remain unchanged.

The Transition

Ten years seems to be the ideal length of a nation's transition period from customary to metric. More than 8 out of 10 manufacturers and 9 out of 10 government agencies think the United States should finish the changeover in ten years or less. Ten years seems to be an ideal compromise: long enough to profitably change machinery when it ages, but not so long that the cost of operating with two systems will offset the savings.

However long it takes to change over, the metric system is definitely coming to the United States. So hang on and brace yourself for some sweeping changes.

2

Events Leading to the Change

Back in the unrecorded history of primitive man, someone, somewhere, measured something for the first time. It probably wasn't much of a measurement. Maybe a caveman stumbled out of his cave one morning and grunted to his wife, "I'll return before the next sunrise," meaning that his trip would take him just far enough so that he could return by the next morning. It wasn't much, but it was one of the most significant measurements in history. Man's intelligence had reached the level where he could measure something.

At first, primitive man kept his measurements simple. He reckoned his hunting trips in the number of days, or "suns," of travel. In this way, he combined distance and time measurements. He had a natural standard against which he could compare his measurements: the length of a day. Later, he used the appearances of the moon to estimate longer times.

His intelligence also awakened to the need to express short lengths. He noticed that everything was relative. His son was one size; he was another; a tree, another. When he saw a child, he might say, "The boy's as tall as my son," even though the child was a bit shorter or taller. His son was the closest comparison he had. And that was good enough for his use.

Later, he refined his measurements. When he draped an animal skin around his body and noticed it was too small or too large, he had made a more accurate estimate of size. When he crept up on a herd of grazing buffalo, he might head for the animal that would provide a fur large enough to drape around his body to keep out the cold winter wind.

These crude estimates and comparisons formed the basis for primitive man's measurements. Soon he grew more aware of the importance of measurements in his life. As limited as his measurements were, they fulfilled his every need.

STANDARDIZED MEASUREMENTS

The first standardized measurements developed at the tribal level and were probably measurements of length. A chief of some tribe may have realized the need for a unit of length after he settled a rash of disputes in his village. He selected some standard length to use as a unit. He might have chosen the length of a sacred rock, a certain animal bone, or

DISTANCE
Measure
FOOT

a part of his body. Human vanity being what it is,
he most often selected a part of his body, probably
his foot.

For the first time, man used a standard of length of his own selection, against which he compared all his measurements. When a member of the tribe wished to make a measurement, the chief compared the length with his foot.

Sooner or later, he tired of loaning out his foot every time someone wanted to make a measurement. So he sat down and whittled a hunk of wood equal in length to his foot. When anyone wanted to make a measurement, the chief gave them the wooden foot. Occasionally, he checked the wooden foot against his own to make sure his foot hadn't grown or that the wooden foot hadn't worn down from overuse.

We can only guess which tribes possessed a system of measurement. Primitive man left few records. The earliest recorded measurements are those of ancient man, around 3000 B. C. By that time, man's measurements had progressed to a high level of sophistication. The crude estimates of primitive man lay centuries behind him.

Ancient man also used units of length that matched parts of the body. Here are a few of the most common:

—The *digit,* the width of a finger.
—The *palm,* the width of four fingers.
—The *span,* the distance between the outstreched thumb and little finger, equal to three palms.
—The *cubit,* equal to the distance from the elbow

to the tip of the middle finger, about six palms.

—The *pace,* equal to a double step, about five feet. One thousand paces by a Roman legionaire was a Roman mile.

—The *fathom,* equal to the distance between the outstretched arms, or four cubits, about six feet.

These units seem crude in comparison with our atomic clocks and space-age precision. But with units such as these, the Egyptians built the Great Pyramid of Cheops (Khufu) with an error of only one part in 4000.

In those days, weight mattered little. Ancient man seldom measured weight accurately. He either counted the number of items he traded, or estimated their value. Most trading was done by barter, so this worked fine.

The Egyptians weighed gold, silver, and jewels. Coined money remained unknown until about 600 B.C., so this weighing was important to high-level transactions. The earliest coins were pieces of gold or silver with the weight stamped on them.

The Greeks adopted the ancient units, then passed them on to the Romans, who spread them throughout Europe in their conquests. The Romans used the base 12 for their foot and pound. This base remains with us today in our unit of length, the foot. The Roman foot and our foot differ by less than 4/10 of an inch. The Romans also gave us the words inch, ounce, and mile.

The oldest known unit of length in England was the *yard* of the Saxon kings. The yard supposedly equalled the length of a sash the king wore around his stomach. The English used this unit long before the year 1000. Later, they set their system of length in five parts:

—The *inch*, equal to the distance across three dry,

round barleycorns placed side by side.

—The *foot,* equal to 12 inches.

—The *yard,* equal to 3 feet.

—The *perch,* equal to 5½ yards.

—The *acre,* the area of a section 40 perches long by 4 perches wide.

Over the years, the English picked up and discarded a confusing array of units. They used the gallon, firkin, pottle, bushel, stake, pail, jackpot, and cartload to measure volume; the clove, stone, wey, last, hundredweight, and sack to measure weight. To further confuse things, they used variations of each unit. A gallon of wine varied from a gallon of ale. A bushel of corn was sold leveled off; a bushel of wheat was sold heaping.

The English and French followed two different courses in solving their measurement problems. England improved on her system. France junked her old system and developed a new system, the metric system.

THE METRIC SYSTEM

The metric system didn't develop from ancient measures and haphazard decrees, as did most systems. It was developed by a group of scientists who carefully studied each new unit.

The urge to change the system of measurement in France stemmed from more than the desire to improve things. The French Revolution triggered a movement to wipe out all traces of the kings and the feudal system. The royal system of measurement stood near the top of the list.

Few of the Revolution's reforms lasted. Their revolutionary calendar, decimal clock, ten-day week, and division of the circle into 100 parts instead of 360 all dropped into oblivion shortly after the government introduced them. But the metric system swept the world. It remains as the most durable of the Revolution's reforms.

The Paris Academy of Sciences developed the system during the 1790's at the request of the French government. The Academy based the system on the meter, a ten-millionth of the distance along a meridian from the equator to the North Pole. Many Frenchmen felt that this was too difficult to understand, unlike units based on a foot or other familiar length. Despite the people's reluctance, the metric system spread throughout France and the rest of the world.

AMERICA'S HERITAGE

We inherited our measurement system from the English. The system is a confusing maze of ancient units. Because of changes after our independence, Great Britain and the United States used slightly different systems. The British ton is 2240 pounds; the ton generally used in the United States is 2000 pounds. In Great Britain, the units of dry and liquid measure were the same. In the United States, the fluid pint, gallon, and quart are used for liquid measurements, the bushel and peck for dry measurements. Of course, these differences became academic when Great Britain began her changeover to the metric system.

The U.S. constitution grants Congress the power to fix the standards of weights and measures. In 1790, Congress asked Secretary of State Thomas Jefferson to study the U.S. measurement system and suggest ways to improve it.

In his report, Jefferson stressed the need for a standard of length. He tried to find a standard in nature, but failed. He doubted that a natural standard of length existed. Instead, he recommended a cylindrical pendulum. When the pendulum was made long enough that it swung from one side to the other and back in exactly two seconds, its length equalled the standard length of Jefferson's proposed system. He divided this length into five "new feet," and each foot into ten "new inches."

In his system, he made fluid and dry measures the same. He developed a system of weight that used a cube of rainwater as the standard. He used decimal relationships for all his units. The nation had just abandoned the farthing, shilling, and pound, and introduced the dollar with its decimal parts. So a decimal system of measurements seemed the next logical step to take. But Jefferson disliked the metric system. He believed his pendulum was better than a French meridian as the standard of length.

Congress studied and discussed Jefferson's report for six years. During that time, France presented us with a copper meter bar and a kilogram standard. She urged us to adopt the metric system. Faced with two proposals, Congressmen did nothing. After a few years, the metric system faded from their memories.

In 1821, Secretary of State John Quincy Adams studied the measurement situation and wrote his *Report Upon Weights and Measures,* an outstanding work on the subject. Of the reasons he listed for the metric system's superiority, three are significant:

—It is based on an invariable length standard taken from nature. (He disagrees with Jefferson here).

—It uses a single unit for weight, and a single unit for liquid and dry capacity measurements.

—It is based on the decimal system.

But Adams objected to the metric system for a number of reasons. For one, he found the meter difficult to estimate, unlike the foot and yard. For another, even the French people hadn't yet accepted the system at that time. And the decimal system had failed to live up to expectations in everyday measurements. To Adams, the base 12 of the English system seemed more useful because it can be divided by 2, 3, 4, and 6. The base 10 of the metric system can be divided by only 2 and 5. Adams recommended

that the English system prevail for the time being, but he left the door open for future improvements.

The Metric System Gains Support

In 1859, the New Hampshire legislature asked Congress to legalize a decimal system of measurements.

In 1860, Maine announced her support for an international system of measurement. Connecticut joined them in 1861.

In 1863, an international postal congress approved the use of the metric system in international postal relations, specifically because of its superiority. They disallowed all other systems.

The same year, Congress created the National Academy of Sciences. From the beginning, the Academy favored the metric system. In 1866, it submitted its first report on the metric system. The chairman of the study committee first emphasized the views of the minority. "The metric system, however, is not considered by many as well adapted to the Anglo-Saxon mind as one which may be devised," he said, "and it was therefore the opinion of a minority of the Academy that, could England and the United States agree upon a system for adoption, it would in all probability in time become universal."

But the majority chose the metric system. Based on the report, Congress acted on two bills and a resolution.

—A resolution to supply each state with a set of metric standards

—A bill to provide metric scales in all post offices dealing with metric countries

—A bill that made it legal to "employ the weights and measures of the metric system" in the United States

The first resolution and bill were minor victories for the metric system. The last bill was the clincher. It would legalize the metric system in the United States for the first time. President Andrew Johnson signed all three laws on July 28, 1866. The third one has since been called the Metric Act of 1866.

The Act hardly affected people's lives. Few Americans knew that Congress had passed such a law. Those who knew didn't really care one way or the other. The law was voluntary. People could ignore it if they wished, and most of them did. Congress had legalized the metric system, but they failed to make its adoption a national policy.

Now that the metric system was legal, many metric supporters lost interest in a changeover. They felt that they had accomplished enough for the time being. The antimetric forces gained a good argument: Anyone who wanted to use the metric system could now do so, legally. If the system was so good, it would soon prove itself.

THE NEW OPPOSITION

After the passage of the Metric Act, some metric supporters regrouped and launched a national campaign for a complete changeover. This campaign triggered the first organized opposition, who fought to retain the customary system. They published pamphlets that attacked the "awful French metric system" on religious grounds, and gave mystic versions of ancient measurements to support their cause. Over the years, supporters and opposition clashed in on-again, off-again battles.

THE TREATY OF THE METER

In 1875, seventeen nations, including the United States, signed the Treaty of the Meter. This historic document created the International Bureau of Weights and Measures in Sevres, France, just outside Paris. The Bureau was to construct new international measurement standards and send copies to participating nations.

The Bureau sent meter bars and kilogram standards to the United States in 1889. In 1893, the Secretary of the Treasury decreed that the new standards were the United States' "fundamental standards" of length and mass. This simple administrative action officially made us a metric nation. From then on, the yard, pound, and other customary units were defined in terms of the metric units.

New associations sprang up either to support or oppose the metric system. The American Metrological Society (from *metrology,* the science of measurement) and the American Metric Bureau topped the list of supporters. On the other side were the American Society of Mechanical Engineers and the International Institute for Preserving and Perfecting Weights and Measures.

The Institute had a fixation for the Egyptian pyramid of King Khufu. They tried to prove that God had directed the Pyramid's building, and it contained all His gifts to mankind. They concluded, in their mysterious way, that this was God's way of showing the superiority of all things Anglo-Saxon, including their measurement system. They begged all good Christians to help fight the alien French metric system.

Toward the end of the nineteenth century, the metric system picked up much support. In 1896, Congress even approved the metric system as the only legal system in the United States, but they returned the bill to committee in one of their well-known turnabouts. The bill lost itself in red tape and was never heard of again.

Past 1902, the battle turned in favor of the antimetric groups. They led such a strong campaign that all bills were bottled up in Congress. Under fire from all sides, the prometric groups retreated and went underground until World War I.

THE NEXT ERA

The American Metric Association was founded in 1916 to meet the antimetric forces in a reopening of the battle. The World Trade Club of San Francisco launched its attack from the West Coast. The Club had a wealthy backer, but his identity remained hidden in the cloak of mystery that surrounded the organization.

The American Institute of Weights and Measures

33

led the antimetric forces. A large group of manufacturers provided its financial backing. As with many groups before it, the Institute mounted its campaign with a flourish. One series of their articles carried such titles as "What Real He-men Think of the Compulsory Metric System," "Metric Chaos in Daily Life," and "A Metric Nightmare."

The experience of American troops in France fueled new interest in the metric system. General John J. Pershing, the commander of American troops, summed up the American metric experience: "The experience of the American Expeditionary Forces in France showed that Americans were able to readily change from our existing weights and measures to the metric system. I think the principal advantages of the metric system are summed up in the fact that this is the only system which has a purely scientific basis. Not the least advantage of the fact that the metric system is based on scientific principles is the facility which that system gives to calculations of all types, from the simplest to the most complex.

"I believe that it would be very desirable to extend the use of the metric system in the United States to the greatest possible extent."

The prometric forces usually stopped here and claimed America's hero's support for their cause. But there was more to his statement. "But I can readily see that there would be many practical obstacles in the attempt entirely to replace our existing system by the metric. . . . as a consequence, I would prefer not to be quoted as advocating the replacement of our present system by the metric system." But he was often quoted, and misquoted, by both sides.

From 1914 to 1933, the nation experienced what has been called "The Great Metric Crusade." Public debate and campaigns reached their highest level on both sides. But again, nothing of significance emerged from Congress.

With the depression, interest in the metric system faded, and with good reason. The major concern of the day was survival and the health—or sickness, if you wish—of the economy. The metric system was pushed aside as the urgent business of feeding a nation was taken care of. The metric system disappeared from the nation's memory.

THE LAST CAMPAIGN

The launching of Russia's Sputnik in 1957 shook the nation. With our honor at stake, we drove forward to pass the Soviet Union in the race to space. Interest in science soared. This activity awakened a new interest in the metric system.

In 1960, an international conference refined the metric system and eliminated slight differences that had developed throughout the world. Members worked out the *International System of Units,* abbreviated *SI* (from its French name, Système International d'Unités), and sometimes called the International Metric System, or just plain metric system.

In 1965, Great Britain signalled her intention to adopt the metric system. Her plan called for a changeover spread over a ten-year period. Her action left us standing alone as the last nation of significance still clinging to the customary system.

Congress passed the Metric Study Act in 1968. The Act directed the Secretary of Commerce to study the metric system and its impact on the nation. The Department assigned the job to the National Bureau of Standards.

The final U.S. Metric Study report was published in July, 1971. The Secretary of Commerce summed up the Study's recommendations:

"That the United States change to the International Metric System deliberately and carefully;

"That this be done through a coordinated national program;

"That the Congress assign the responsibility for guiding the change . . . to a central coordinating body responsive to all sectors of our society . . .

"That early priority be given to educating every American schoolchild and the public at large to think in metric terms;

"That immediate steps be taken by the Congress to foster U.S. participation in international standards activities;

"That in order to encourage efficiency and minimize the overall costs to society, the general rule should be that any changeover costs shall 'lie where they fall';

"That the Congress ... establish a target date ten years ahead, by which time the U.S. will have become predominantly, though not exclusively, metric;

"That there be a firm government commitment to this goal."

The stage has been set for the changeover. After centuries of debate, we are on our way to becoming a truly metric nation for the first time.

3

The Metric System

One advantage of the metric system is its use of a single unit for every quantity. To form fractions and multiples of a unit, you use a prefix that is an even power of ten. Here is a list of the prefixes.

PREFIXES FOR SI UNITS

PREFIX	SYMBOL	MULTIPLICATION FACTOR	POWER OF TEN
tera	T	1,000,000,000,000	10^{12}
giga	G	1,000,000,000	10^{9}
mega	M	1,000,000	10^{6}
kilo	k	1,000	10^{3}
hecto	h	100	10^{2}
deka	da	10	10
deci	d	.1	10^{-1}
centi	c	.01	10^{-2}
milli	m	.001	10^{-3}
micro	μ	.000001	10^{-6}
nano	n	.000000001	10^{-9}

PREFIX	SYMBOL	MULTIPLICATION FACTOR	POWER OF TEN
pico	p	.000000000001	10^{-12}
femto	f	.000000000000001	10^{-15}
atto	a	.000000000000000001	10^{-18}

You can use the prefixes with all metric units. When you need a quantity larger or smaller than the basic unit, just tack on a prefix at the beginning. The meter, for example, is the basic metric unit of length. You can express the distance between two cities as 15,000 meters, or you can slip the decimal point three places to the left, add the prefix *kilo,* and express the distance as 15 kilometers.

kilo = 1000
1 kilometer = 1000 meters
15 kilometers = 15,000 meters

If your finger measures .075 meters in length, move the decimal point two places to the right, add the prefix *centi,* and express the length as 7.5 centimeters.

centi = .01
1 centimeter = .01 meters
7.5 centimeters = .075 meters

In the customary system, you can't easily convert 15,000 yards to miles; you must divide by 1760. Nor can you easily convert .075 yards to inches; you must multiply by 36.

THE METRIC UNITS

The metric system is based on the units of length, mass, and time. Scientists regard these units as the heart of any measurement system. Four more basic units, a couple of supplementary units, and many derived units make up the rest of the system. Derived units are formed from the basic units and other derived units. Here are the most common metric units. (Conversion factors for converting from customary to metric units are listed after Chapter 7.)

COMMON METRIC UNITS

QUANTITY	UNIT	SYMBOL
(BASIC UNITS)		
Length	meter	m
Mass	kilogram	kg
Time	second	s
Electric current	ampere	A
Temperature	kelvin	K
	or Celsius	C
(DERIVED UNITS)		
Area	square meter	m^2
	or hectare	ha
	(unofficial)	

QUANTITY	UNIT	SYMBOL
	(DERIVED UNITS)	
Volume or capacity	cubic meter	m³
	or liter	l
	(unofficial)	
Frequency	hertz	Hz
Velocity	meter per second	m/s (km/hr commonly used)
Force	newton	N
Energy	joule	J
Pressure	newton per square meter	N/m²
	or pascal	P
Power	watt	W
Voltage	volt	V
	(SUPPLEMENTARY UNIT)	
Angle	radian	rad

Remember that to make multiples or fractions of these units, just add the proper prefix at the beginning.

LENGTH

The *meter* (sometimes spelled *metre)* is the basic unit of length in the metric system. A meter is about three inches longer than a yard. For measurements of longer length, you can use the *kilometer,* about 6/10 of a mile. For shorter lengths, use the *centimeter,* about 4/10 of an inch. A five-cent piece measures

41

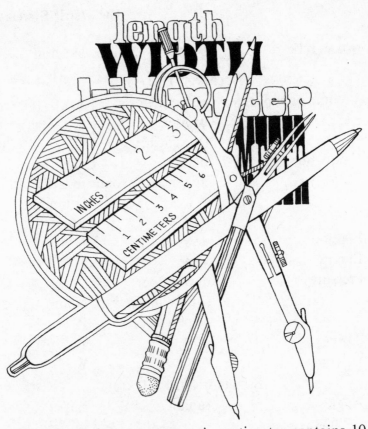

about 2 centimeters across. A centimeter contains 10 *millimeters.*

1 meter (m) = 3.3 feet or 39.4 inches
1 kilometer (km) = 1000 meters; 1 mile = 1.6 km
1 centimeter = .01 meters; 1 inch = 2.5 cm
1 millimeter = .001 meters; 1 inch = 25.4 mm

A "metric ruler" of 30 centimeters is almost the

same length as a 12-inch ruler. On double-edged rulers, you will find the metric measures on the "other edge," opposite the inch markings. A "meter stick" measures a meter in length. It will replace the yard-stick.

The meter will replace many familiar units. Among these are the inch, foot, yard, statute mile, nautical mile, link, chain, caliber, fathom, micron, and mil. The nautical mile equals a minute of latitude on maps, so it is important to navigation. It may remain with us longer than any of the other units.

APPROXIMATE HEIGHT EQUIVALENTS

If your height is:	In metric, it's:
4'	122 cm
4'1"	124 cm
4'2"	127 cm
4'3"	130 cm
4'4"	132 cm
4'5"	135 cm
4'6"	137 cm
4'7"	140 cm
4'8"	142 cm
4'9"	145 cm
4'10"	147 cm
4'11"	150 cm
5'	152 cm
5'1"	155 cm

If your height is:	In metric, it's:
5'2"	157 cm
5'3"	160 cm
5'4"	163 cm
5'5"	165 cm
5'6"	168 cm
5'7"	170 cm
5'8"	173 cm
5'9"	175 cm
5'10"	178 cm
5'11"	180 cm
6'	183 cm
6'1"	185 cm
6'2"	188 cm

MASS

Few things confuse science students more than the difference between weight and mass. The customary system's use of the pound for both weight and mass has caused part of this confusion. Mass is the amount of matter, or "stuff," in an object. Weight is the force gravity exerts on that object. An astronaut possesses the same mass on the moon as he does on earth, but because of the difference in gravity, his weight differs considerably. On the moon, he weighs only 1/6 of what he does on earth, because the force of gravity on the moon is 1/6 of earth's.

In the metric system, mass is expressed in *kilograms* (or other multiples of the gram). Force is expressed in *newtons*. Weight is a force, so we should also express it in newtons. However, since all of our everyday measurements are made on earth, weight is related to mass, and metric scales are calibrated in kilograms. When we say something "weighs" 5 kilograms, we actually mean it has a mass of 5 kilograms.

A kilogram (kg) equals slightly over 2 pounds. Smaller masses use the gram. The kilogram is divided into 1000 grams (kilo being the prefix for 1000). A gram is about the mass of 3 aspirins. A five-cent piece has a mass of five grams. The gram and kilogram will handle all of our everyday weight measurements, from a package of butter (a few hundred grams) to a person (a 150-pound man is 68 kilograms). Larger masses use the *metric ton*, equal to 1000 kilograms. A medium-sized car has a mass of about a metric ton.

APPROXIMATE CONVERSIONS

1 kg = 2.2 pounds; 1 pound = .45 kg
1 ounce = 28 grams

After the changeover to metric, the ounce, pound, long ton, short ton, assay ton, grain, dram, hundredweight, pennyweight, and slug will become obsolete.

APPROXIMATE MASS EQUIVALENTS

If you weigh this many pounds:	Your equivalent in kilograms is:
60	27
65	29
70	32
75	34
80	36
85	39
90	41
95	43
100	45
105	48
110	50
115	52
120	54
125	57
130	59
135	61
140	64
145	66
150	68
155	70
160	73
165	75
170	77
175	79

180	82
185	84
190	86
195	88
200	91

TIME

The *second* continues as the basic SI unit of time. Although SI doesn't list the minute, hour, day, week, month, and year, you couldn't get along without them. They will remain a part of your life.

CAPACITY

Capacity, or volume, measures the amount of material that can fill a container. Capacity in the metric system is measured in *cubic meters*. A box one meter on each side has a volume of one cubic meter. The *cubic centimeter*, sometimes abbreviated *cc*, is the volume of a container one centimeter on each side. The medical field often uses the cubic centimeter.

The *liter* is a more convenient unit for everyday use. The liter contains slightly more than a quart. It's equal to 1000 cc, the volume of a container one decimeter (1/10 meter, about 4 inches) on each side. For this reason, it's sometimes called a cubic decimeter. A liter of water weighs about a kilogram, or 2.2 pounds.

When bottlers label their product's contents in metric units, they commonly use *centiliters*, abbreviated cl. A liter contains 100 centiliters. A centiliter equals about 2 teaspoons. Smaller volumes use the *milliliter* (ml). One teaspoon contains about 5 ml. A milliliter is the same as a cubic centimeter.

APPROXIMATE CONVERSIONS

1 liter = 1.06 quarts; 1 quart = .95 liter
1 liter = 100 centiliters; 1 fluid ounce = 3 cl
1 liter = 1000 milliliters; 1 fluid ounce = 30 ml

The SI capacity units will replace the fluid ounce, pint, quart, gallon, barrel, bushel, peck, and gill.

AREA

In the customary system, areas are measured in acres or square feet. In the metric system, small areas are measured in *square meters*, large areas in *hectares (ha)*. The hectare isn't an official SI unit, but it's used in all metric countries. A hectare equals 10,000 square meters, or the area of a square 100 meters on each side.

APPROXIMATE CONVERSIONS

1 square meter (m^2) = 1.2 square yards
1 hectare = 2.5 acres; 1 acre = .4 ha
1 square kilometer = 100 ha; 1 square mile = 260 ha

TEMPERATURE

In the customary system, we measure temperature in degrees Fahrenheit. The boiling point of water is 212° and its freezing point is 32°. The SI unit of temperature is the *kelvin*. The Kelvin scale starts at absolute zero, the point where there is no heat at all. Absolute zero on the Fahrenheit scale is 459.6 degrees below zero.

The Kelvin scale is useful for scientists, but it is impractical for everyday use. SI has adopted the degree Celsius for everyday use. Formerly called the centigrade scale, the Celsius thermometer uses 0° as the freezing point of water and 100° as the boiling point. A degree Celsius is the same amount as a kelvin, but the Celsius scale starts at a different point.

The degree Celsius and the degree Fahrenheit are related by a formula. To convert from Celsius (or centigrade) degrees to Fahrenheit degrees, multiply by 9/5 and add 32; to convert Fahrenheit degrees to Celsius degrees, subtract 32 and multiply by 5/9. For example, to find the equivalent of 77 degrees Fahrenheit, first subtract 32 from 77 to get 45. Multiply by 5/9 to get the answer, 25 degrees Celsius.

A normal body temperature of 98.6 degrees Fahrenheit measures about 37 degrees Celsius. If the temperature outside reaches 25 degrees Celsius, wear your summer clothes.

APPROXIMATE COMPARISONS

degrees Fahrenheit	degrees Celsius
0	–18
32	0
40	4.4
50	10
60	16
70	21
80	27
90	32
100	38

SPEED

The customary system measures speed, or velocity, in miles per hour. In the metric system, speed is measured in *kilometers per hour*. To convert, use the same conversions as between kilometers and miles.

APPROXIMATE CONVERSIONS

1 kilometer per hour (km/hr) = .6 miles per hour
1 mile per hour = 1.6 km/hr (also abbreviated *kph*)

OTHER UNITS

Here is a list of other units that will affect you.

Power—SI uses the *watt* as its unit of power, so

the ratings of light bulbs and stereo amplifiers will remain the same. The horsepower will be abandoned.

Frequency—The SI unit of frequency is the *hertz*, which replaced the cycle-per-second a few years ago. Radio stations announce their broadcast frequencies in *kilohertz* or *megahertz*. AM stations broadcast from about 535 to 1605 kilohertz, and FM stations from 88 to 108 megahertz. Electrical appliances ordinarily require power with a frequency of 60 hertz.

Voltage—SI uses the *volt*, so the batteries you buy for your flashlight and radio will be rated the same as they are now.

Current—The *ampere* is also an SI unit. Fuses will be rated the same as before, in amperes.

Energy—The SI unit of energy is the *joule*. The joule will replace many familiar units, including the calorie, British Thermal Unit, kilowatt-hour, erg, and the nuclear ton equivalent of TNT.

The abandonment of the calorie may confuse dieters, who will have to lower their "joule intake" rather than their calorie intake. But whether they cut joules or calories is unimportant; they will still be just as hungry at bedtime.

Electrical companies measure the amount of electrical energy we consume in kilowatt-hours. They prefer to retain the kilowatt-hour, even though it isn't an SI unit. The National Bureau of Standards says the kilowatt-hour must go. Only time will tell who will win the struggle. A kilowatt-hour is 3,600,000 joules or 3.6 megajoules.

Pressure—Pressure is the force over a certain area. The customary unit of pressure is the pound per square inch, or psi. The SI unit is the *newton per square meter*, also called a *pascal*.

4

How Will It Affect You?

Under the metric system, stores will sell onions by the kilogram, milk by the liter, and wire by the meter. These are some of the changes that will disrupt your life. The list goes on and on.

IN THE MARKETPLACE

Some of the first changes will surface in the super-markets. Products now sold in customary units will be sold in metric units that are approximately the same. The metric system will affect almost every product sold.

Products now sold by the fluid ounce, pint, quart, and gallon will be sold by the liter or centiliter. Shoppers will buy as many liters of milk and juice as they now do quarts. Since a liter contains 6 per cent more than a quart, sales should rise by 6 per cent.

The opposite happened in countries where the liter measures less than the Imperial quart that had been in use. When dairy companies reduced the size of their milk bottles to one liter, milk sales dropped by the amount of the difference between the two sizes.

Products now sold by the pint will be sold in 50-centiliter bottles or cans. Gallon jugs and cans will increase to four liters, the closest equivalent to our present four quarts to a gallon. Here are a few of the products the metric system will affect:

> Milk and ice cream
> Paint
> Glue
> Cooking and vegetable oil
> Some fruits, such as strawberries
> Some seafoods, such as oysters and clams
> Fruit and vegetable juices
> Wine, liquor, and beer
> Soft drinks
> Mayonnaise and salad dressing
> Pickles and relishes
> Liquid detergents
> Bath products and grooming aids, such as mouthwash, hair tonic, shampoo, perfume, and after-shave lotion
> Liquid seasonings, such as hot pepper sauce and soy sauce

Liquid medicine, such as cough syrup

All other products whose labels now give the contents in fluid ounces, pints, quarts, gallons, bushels, pecks, or other volume measurement

If the change in capacity units will disrupt the markets, the change in weight units will revolutionize them. Most food products in the stores are sold by weight. The list includes almost everything worth eating, and then some.

Meat

Fresh vegetables, such as potatoes and onions

Fresh fruit

Cheese

Canned goods sold by weight, such as vegetables, fruit, peanuts, and meat

Packaged goods sold by weight, such as potato chips, flour, rice, spaghetti, macaroni, crackers, cookies, and dry dog food

Some bottled items, such as baby food, catsup, and olives

Packaged detergents and starch

Aerosol spray cans

Some bath items, such as bath powder, soap, and toothpaste

All products whose labels list the contents in pounds or ounces

Products the supermarkets either package themselves or sell loose will present few problems. Meat is one example. Supermarkets will still sell meat in the same easy-to-serve cuts. The same price will appear on the label. But the weight will appear in kilograms. Suppose spareribs sell at $1.00 a pound. On a 2.2-pound package, the label will list the price as $2.20. When the market sells meat by the kilogram, the label will look like this:

1 kg $2.20 per kg   Total cost: $2.20

A package of 2.2 pounds of spare ribs at $1.00 a pound costs the same as one kilogram at $2.20 a kilogram. A kilogram equals 2.2 pounds. If a shopper wished, she could ignore the units of measurement, pay her $2.20, and take her spare ribs home with no more fuss, bother, or kilograms.

Fresh vegetables and fruits will weather the change as well as meat. Supermarkets will sell onions, potatoes, and the like in even metric sizes. Instead of five-pound bags of onions, they can sell two-kilogram (4.4 pounds) or 2.5-kilogram (5.5 pounds) bags. These "metric bags" are within an onion or two of the five-pound bag. Markets can do the same thing with other sizes. Five kilograms make a fine substitute for ten pounds; 500 grams for a pound; 250 grams for half-a-pound.

Markets will breeze through the change to metric units. They will buy metric scales and train employees to handle the new units, but that is about all that will be necessary. They can handle the price change from pounds to kilograms as easily as they now handle their daily price changes.

The changeover will give supermarkets the chance to increase their sales of items sold by weight, in the same way that they will increase their milk sales. For one example, they can sell five-kilogram bags instead of ten-pound bags. A five-kilogram bag of potatoes contains about 11 pounds, 10 per cent more than a ten-pound bag. So if the supermarket sells the same number of bags, their sales will rise 10 per cent. This approach is an honest one; you will receive all you pay for. And a five-kilogram bag of potatoes makes more sense in a metric society than a ten-pound bag.

The greatest changes will appear on the shelves, in the bottled, packaged, and canned goods. Most of these are sold by weight. Soon, more and more products will list their contents in both systems. One by one, producers will drop the customary units and label only in metric units. Later, they will sell "metric bottles," "metric packs," and "metric cans," all scaled to even kilograms or liters. By the end of the transition period, almost all products will either be metric or will give the contents only in metric units.

Producers who refuse to produce metric products will run into problems. Customers and consumer groups will complain that the odd sizes confuse them and make cost comparisons difficult. A change to metric would eliminate these complaints.

When markets change to metric units, they could maneuver prices to hide an increase. If onions cost

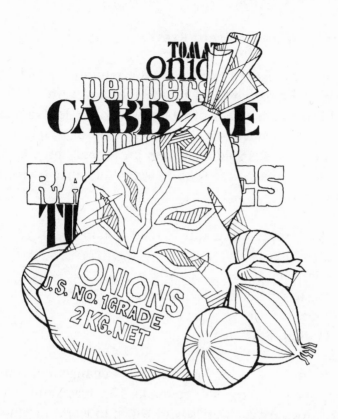

15 cents a pound, they should cost about 33 cents a kilogram. Some supermarkets might round this off to 35 cents, a hidden 6 per cent increase. Steak that costs $2.00 a pound should run to approximately $4.41 a kilogram. If a supermarket charges $4.50, they will ring up an extra 2 per cent profit. Few customers keep close enough track of prices to notice the difference. However, Congress or local governments could pass laws to prevent businesses from slipping in a price increase when they change to metric units.

The changeover will also affect products sold by length. Items now sold by the foot and yard will be sold by the meter. Your family will feel less impact here than with items sold by capacity or weight because products sold by length are usually purchased less often than those sold by weight or capacity. Here are a few:

Wire, rope, string, thread, and ribbon
Dental floss
Cloth
Waxed paper and foil wrap
Pipe
Garden hose

Products sold by the piece won't change, but some improvements can still be made. The dozen and gross are awkward quantities with which to work. Products now sold by the dozen could better be sold in units of ten. Computations would be easier, and the new unit would conform to the decimal metric system, our money system, and our system of counting. Try to figure out how many eggs are in 14 dozen or how much an egg costs if a dozen costs 89 cents, and you will realize the difficulty of using the dozen. If a box of 10 eggs costs 89 cents, just slip the decimal point one place left and arrive at a cost of 8.9 cents an

60

egg. Fourteen boxes with ten eggs inside each one total 140 eggs. Since the metric prefix for 10 is deka, the new unit could be called the *dekon.*

The gross is another leftover from a more confusing era. A gross equals a dozen dozens, or 144. A unit of 100 would simplify things. Since the metric prefix for 100 is hecto, the new unit might be called the *hecton.*

Items sold by the piece are numerous. They chew up a sizable chunk of a family's budget. Here are a few of the most common:

Eggs

Bakery products, such as rolls, donuts, and cupcakes

Paper products, such as facial tissue, toilet tissue, and napkins

Teabags

Products with a specific number of items inside, such as chewing gum (five sticks) and photographic film (20 or 36 exposures for one common type).

Products sold by the piece may be labelled in other units. A box of donuts may be labeled in grams or kilograms instead of ounces or pounds; a package of toilet tissue may list its length on the package.

DRIVING WON'T BE THE SAME

Speed limits on our roads will be posted in kilometers per hour. A seventy-mile-per-hour speed limit is about 113 kilometers per hour. Authorities will round this off to 110 or 115 kph. A car's speedometer gives the speed in miles per hour. A driver must divide the metric speed limit by 1.6 to get miles per hour, a difficult task while driving. To make things smoother, authorities will probably post speed limits in both systems for awhile—at least until speedometers are changed over to show kilometers.

Road signs will display the distance to the next town in kilometers. Again, you must divide by 1.6 to get the distance in miles. The state of Ohio already lists the distances in both systems on their road signs, and other states will begin to do the same.

Automobile manufacturers will change the speedometers of their cars to kilometers per hour. During the transition, their speedometers might display the speed in both systems. After a few years, the mph markings could be dropped.

Nuts and bolts on cars will change to even metric sizes, as they are on foreign cars. Other critical sizes, such as engine capacity, might change to even metric dimensions. Spark plug threads and bearings are already metric-sized.

Tire manufacturers will measure their tires in metric units. On a 7.50 x 14 tire, the wheel rim diameter

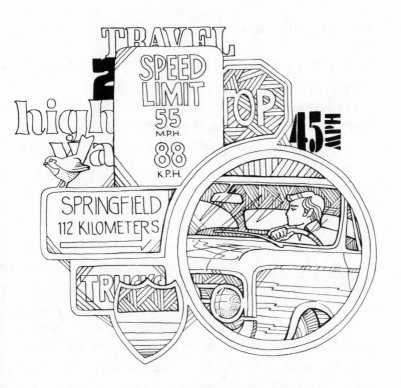

is 14 inches and the tire width is about 7.5 inches. The metric equivalent is 19.05 by 35.6 centimeters. Tire manufacturers will probably round this off to 19 x 36.

If the family car uses any gauges to monitor engine performance, these will also change. Oil pressure gauges won't display pressure in pounds per square inch, but in pascals. SI uses the ampere, so car ammeters will remain the same. A tachometer measures revolutions per minute, a unit that is the same in all systems, so tachometers won't change either. Gas gauges that indicate gasoline level in fractions of a tank will stay the same. They would change only if they gave gasoline level directly in gallons.

Gasoline stations will sell gasoline and oil by the liter, instead of by the gallon and quart. The change will be smooth and gradual. Customers either buy a few dollars worth, or "fill 'er up." Either way, the pump gives the price of the gas sold to the customer. He can pay this amount and ignore the number of liters he bought, if he wishes.

We judge a car's performance partly by the horsepower of its engine. The horsepower equals 746 watts. Since SI has doomed the horsepower, auto dealers must find another way to impress you with a car's performance. They could claim that their new model has a powerful 200-kilowatt engine under the hood. But the watt is an electrical unit to most of us. It would sound alien if someone used it to describe a car's engine.

Gas mileage is measured in miles per gallon. The mile will change to the kilometer, the gallon to the liter. So gasoline consumption (don't call it mileage anymore) will be measured in kilometers per liter. The conversion factor is .425. Ten miles per gallon is 4.25 kilometers per liter.

HOME, SWEET HOME

At home, you will notice the first changes on radio and TV. Announcers will give measurements in both

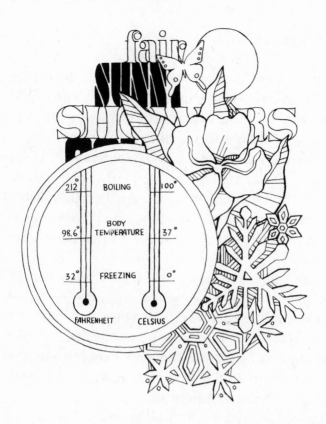

systems, or only in the metric system. The TV weather girl will reel off the day's temperatures in degrees Celsius, rainfall in centimeters, and wind velocity in kilometers per hour.

Someday, all thermometers on the market will measure in degrees Celsius. Manufacturers could produce thermometers that give the temperature in both systems. But households seldom buy a thermometer, so little would be gained. By the time most persons break their medical thermometer, they will already know the degree Celsius. Mothers will soon enough learn that when a child's temperature reaches 41 degrees Celsius, it's long past the time to see a doctor.

Stoves will indicate the oven temperature in degrees Celsius. Publishers will revise their cookbooks to indicate the new temperatures. At first, they will give temperatures in both systems. Later, they will drop the obsolete degrees Fahrenheit and give only degrees Celsius.

Pots, pans, and bowls will change to metric sizes, but only over a long period. Housewives will buy metric-sized kitchenware only when the old pots and pans wear out. Since a quart and a liter are almost the same, a housewife couldn't care less whether a saucepan can hold a liter or a quart. In the kitchen, she can ignore the difference.

Cups, tablespoons, and teaspoons as measures will change to metric sizes. Two proposals have been suggested. Both retain the present relationship between the three measures. Three teaspoons make one tablespoon; 16 tablespoons make one cup. One cup measures 236.6 milliliters.

One proposal sets the "metricup" at 240 ml. The teaspoon would measure an even 5 ml; the tablespoon, 15 ml. This makes everything even except the relationship between the liter and the cup. A 250-ml cup measures exactly ¼ liter, a more even relationship.

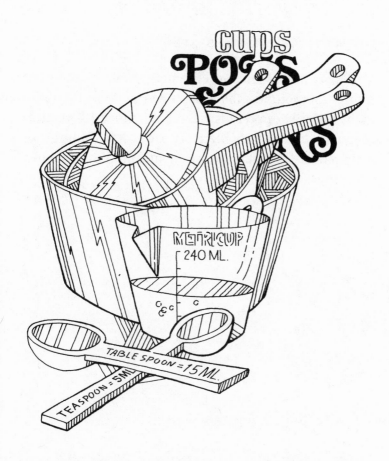

But the tablespoon here would contain 15.6 ml; the teaspoon, 5.2 ml.

Yardsticks and rulers will disappear from the house. Meter sticks and 30-cm rulers will replace them. Tape measures will measure in meters, subdivided into centimeters and millimeters.

Manufacturers will rate refrigerators in cubic meters of capacity, instead of cubic feet. The changeover will give them the chance to eliminate some meaningless ratings. Sometimes, they rate a refrigerator's capacity in the number of pounds it can hold. Since 150 pounds of meat differs considerably from 150 pounds of whipped cream, this rating is meaningless to most consumers.

5

The Impact on Business and Labor

The changeover to the metric system will affect American industry more than any other group. Industry faces billions of dollars in costs and a flood of problems. Since most Americans work at jobs in private industry, the changeover will affect them as much at work as it will at home.

THE PROBLEMS OF INDUSTRY

The costs of going metric will hurt industry more than anything else. Estimates have run from $25 billion to $50 billion, although these are probably exaggerated. With a ten-year transition period, the costs should run far below estimates. Good planning and preparation will keep costs low.

Industry will face other problems besides cost. Here are a few.

Safety—Workers will be unfamiliar with the metric system. When they convert between metric and cus-

69

tomary units, they could make mistakes and cause accidents. A truck driver may err when he converts a speed limit from kilometers per hour to miles per hour, and drive too fast. A worker may misadjust a new metric machine and injure himself.

Machinery replacement—Industry can adjust or modify many of their machines to metric sizes. In time, other machines will wear out and industry can replace them with metric machines. They may have to spend millions to replace the machines that remain. They anticipate problems with obtaining parts and tools during the transition period.

Inventories—Some businesses will have to stock a dual inventory of products: one in SI sizes, the other in customary. Some manufacturers must also produce their products in two sizes, called dual dimensioning. Engineering standards, designs, and drawings for their products will change. The changeover will affect different industries in different ways. Canners might stock a dual inventory only during part of the transition period. Afterwards, they can close down their customary production line and produce only metric cans. Suppliers of parts for ships, on the other hand, may have to stock a dual inventory for twenty-five years, since ships usually stay in service that long.

Retraining—Everyone from file clerk to president will have to learn to apply the metric system to his job. The burden of training will fall on industry. The

70

"loss of experience" mentioned earlier is an example where retraining can help the worker adjust.

Managers will require retraining as much as workers do. A manager might be capable of deciding in a moment to buy 500 short tons of copper at $1200 a ton, but he may hesitate when offered it at $1300 a metric ton, a real bargain. He must make a calculation to see if the price is right. If he miscalculates, he might miss a bargain, or pay too high a price.

Metric imports—Imports will increase, but only slightly. Some foreign companies can't sell us their metric products now because American buyers prefer customary sizes. After the changeover, they can compete with American companies. Others can shut down the production lines they maintain for customary-sized products. Their costs will drop, and they can sell their products at a lower price. Fortunately, an increase in the sale of American metric products abroad should offset these imports.

Other problems—Many problems and costs will be hidden. Loss of time, confusion, damage to machinery, and lower product quality will add millions of dollars to the cost of going metric. Management will know little about these costs. The extra costs will lose themselves in the normal confusion of running a corporation.

After the dust settles, industry will benefit from the changeover. They can stop dual dimensioning, calculations will be simpler, and they can communicate more easily with their foreign customers. They can also eliminate useless product sizes. In Great Britain, one ball-bearing manufacturer replaced 280 old sizes with 30 metric sizes. Clothing manufacturers hope to make some sense out of the way they now size clothes by adopting an internationally-accepted method based on the metric system.

Each industry will deal with its own set of problems. Here are a few industries and the effect on each.

Electronics—Most electronic units are already SI, so the industry will feel only a few changes. Some basic units will affect the industry slightly. They will sell electrical wire by the meter instead of the foot, and surplus equipment by the kilogram instead of the pound.

Construction—The construction industry expects a few problems, especially with training of workers, and dual inventories. Present sizes of wallboard, plywood panels, and cement blocks are close to metric sizes. Manufacturers can easily change them. Construction workers should easily adapt to the new sizes.

Shipping—Metric nations build most of the world's ships. Marine engines are built to metric standards. The United States trades more with metric nations than with any other. So the maritime and shipping industries welcome the changeover. They do expect a major problem in the supply of spare parts. The

72

average life of a merchant ship is twenty-five years. Suppliers may hesitate to stock customary parts that long.

Home appliances—Companies with foreign operations already produce products in both systems. The industry worries that performance claims in metric units will confuse their customers. But shoppers understand few performance claims, and pay attention to them even less. The industry also fears competition from foreign metric products. This competition is already so severe, however, that a metric changeover could hardly worsen things.

Automobiles—One out of every three cars sold in 1973 featured metric parts. Ford operates the first metric engine plant in the United States at Lima, Ohio. The plant will build a four-cylinder engine to metric standards. Since the industry does a large chunk of their business overseas, they are accustomed to dealing with metric units.

Textiles—This industry's main problems are employee training and machinery replacement. Pattern cutters may have to learn to cut patterns from metric-sized bolts of cloth. Plant employees who do piece work may find their incomes reduced while they struggle with the new system.

Soft drinks—The soft drink industry favors the customary system, but they can readjust machines to fill metric-sized bottles with few problems. They do worry about the billions of returnable and reusable containers, though. The industry would suffer high costs in discarding all the old customary-sized bottles and replacing them with metric-sized ones. Perhaps a means of recycling will be the answer.

Airlines—The world's airlines use many customary units. An airplane's altitude is measured in feet, its rate of climb is in feet per second, and its speed is in knots (a nautical mile per hour). Many engine parts are scaled to customary sizes. Each aircraft mechanic has a tool kit full of customary tools. Aircraft instruments, such as oil pressure gages, indicate in customary units. Navigational aids give their information in customary units. So a metric changeover will cause many problems. To prevent chaos, the world's governments and airlines will cooperate during the transition period. To avoid accidents, pilots and aircraft controllers must learn the metric units well.

Hospitals—Hospitals presently use the metric units extensively because the drug and medical fields use them so much. The changeover will cause few problems.

Small business—Small businesses will follow the lead of government and industry. Since they lack the money to change over at short notice, small businesses will feel the effect more than most others. If they must change too soon or too fast, many could be forced into bankruptcy. Again, good planning is a must.

The Impact on Business and Labor

America's employees will face two major problems:
1. Replacement of tools.
2. Learning the metric units.

Auto mechanics, plumbers, and other tradesmen will have to buy metric tools. Depending on the trade, the cost will run from a few cents for a metric ruler to $1000 or more for a metric tool kit. Some unions grumble about this extra expense for their members. They reject the philosophy of "letting the costs lie where they fall," and may insist that employers replace the employees' tools.

Most tradesmen exaggerate their tool replacement costs. During a ten-year transition period, many tools will wear out or be lost and require replacement anyway.

Unions may also demand that employees retrain older workers in the use of metric units. New graduates of technical schools will handle the metric units with ease, but older workers will know only the customary units or will be slow to learn the new ones. Because of this advantage, younger workers may outperform older workers for awhile. Those who refuse to learn the metric units will fall behind.

Here are a few trades and professions, and the effect on each.

Architects and construction workers—The construction industry experiences a high turnover of employees. Workers constantly move in and out of the industry. New workers will know few metric units and must be trained. Skilled workers, such as masons, carpenters, and electricians, will need some metric tools. Most architects support the metric changeover.

Lawyers—Lawyers use the customary system in almost all their cases. They encounter the metric system in a few cases, usually when they deal with scientific documents. More than any other group, they see the problems ahead in changing thousands of local, state, and federal laws and tariffs to metric units.

Dentists, doctors, and nurses—Dentists use metric units often, so they expect few problems. The medical field uses a mixture of units. Metric units are used in medical research; drugs are dispensed in metric units; doctors record the patient's height and weight in customary units. Doctors and nurses have supported the metric changeover for years.

Scientists—Most branches of science have used the metric system for years. But applied biology, environmental sciences, and a few others use customary units, so they will experience problems, especially with records and textbooks.

Engineers—Engineers apply scientific discoveries to everyday life, so most engineers already know and use the metric system. Associations of agricultural, chemical, civil, mining, metallurgical, petroleum, electronic, and mechanical engineers welcome the changeover.

76

6

The Impact on Government and Education

Among the nations of the world, the United States is unique. Unlike other nations, ours has an assortment of many governments, all separate from each other. We have city governments, county governments, state governments, a federal government, and even commonwealth and territorial governments. In other nations, the national government makes all important decisions and enforces all major laws. Local governments administer local affairs and follow the orders of the national government.

The U.S. constitution says, "The powers not delegated to the United States . . . are reserved to the States respectively, or to the people." Neither Congress nor the President will force the people to use the metric system. They will simply try to persuade us to use it. The federal government will use the power of the law only in certain cases, such as product labeling. So the metric changeover in America requires the joint effort of all levels of government, from the smallest city government to the President of the United States.

THE STATES AND CITIES

Most state governments look forward to the metric changeover, even though they face many problems. For one, they must change all of their highway speed limit and distance signs. Ohio got a head start and added metric equivalents to many of their signs. One Ohio highway distance sign now reads:

CLEVELAND
94 MILES
151 KILOMETERS

States will have to rewrite many laws. In vehicle repair, building maintenance, and inventories, they face the same problems as industry.

City governments expect problems in law enforcement, fire protection, and public works. They will change speed limit signs, rewrite traffic laws, and change building and fire codes. Designs of sewers, buildings, and other construction will change when building materials and standards change to metric.

THE FEDERAL GOVERNMENT

The federal government is the largest employer in the nation. More than 5.5 million people draw federal salary checks. With so many people, the federal government faces its major problems with its employees. Many will resist the change or refuse to learn the new units. Since the federal government will lead the nation toward a metric changeover, its employees should be among the first to learn the metric units.

Here are some other problems federal agencies have said they expect to encounter:

Confusion—The metric units will confuse the older employees, who could make costly and dangerous mistakes.

Dual inventories—The U.S. goverment maintains one of the world's largest stocks of spare parts and supplies. In millions of square meters of warehouse space all over the world, they stock hundreds of thousands of items, from anchors to zucchini. If they stock a dual inventory on even a small percentage of these items, the cost could run to billions of dollars.

Equipment replacement—The government will have to replace millions of dollars of equipment, machinery, and measuring equipment.

Laws—Many federal laws and tariffs will change. A ten-year transition period will allow plenty of time to do this. Problems could arise in the field, where agents who are unfamiliar with the metric units try to enforce the new laws.

Costs—Around 1971, the federal government estimated that a metric changeover would cost its agencies $580 million over ten years. This "bargain price" works out to about 28 cents a year for every person in the United States.

THE MILITARY

American industry supplies the armed forces' equipment and hardware. Electronic companies design the Army's radio communications systems, shipbuilders turn out the Navy's nuclear submarines, and construction firms build the soldier's barracks. The armed forces must work closely with industry during the metric system transition period. In some cases, such as the changeover of aircraft navigational aids, the armed forces and industry will face the same problems.

The armed forces already use metric units in air support, mapping, infared, ranging devices, and air and road distances. A general will order his troops to advance eight kilometers to hill 304, a hill 304 meters high. They also use metric measurements in much of their armament, such as the 20 mm cannon and 7.63 mm machine gun.

Some of their problems, such as dual inventories and equipment replacement, are covered in the section on the federal government. Here are a few more.

Costs—The Department of Defense has estimated their changeover costs at over $18 billion, according to a survey made by the U. S. Metric Study. This includes only the costs they can easily estimate, such as training and dual inventories. They couldn't estimate the hidden costs of confusion, mistakes, and equipment damage. A mechanic who tries to fit a metric-sized part in a customary-sized hole could ruin an engine. A government buyer who makes an error when he converts from feet to meters could order a 500-year supply of telephone wire by mistake.

Training and safety—In some cases, personnel must be trained to use the metric units so well that they will respond without hesitation. An air traffic controller who hesitates for a moment could cause an airplane to crash. A pilot who erroneously converts meters to feet might drop his bomb load on a group of friendly soldiers.

Supply—Of all things the armed forces of any nation need to survive, supplies and spare parts rank as one of the most important. Lack of supplies can ground an air force and disable a naval fleet. The temporary confusion of a metric changeover could disrupt this supply.

A metric changeover will benefit the armed forces in many ways. They can reduce some supply inventories, make computations faster, and communicate better with our allies.

EDUCATION

The success of a metric changeover rests with the

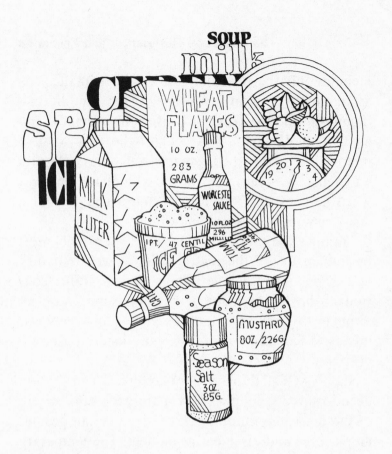

schools. They will prepare American youth to handle the new units. A good educational program will assure a smooth transition; a poor program, a chaotic transition.

Educators say that the two main advantages of the customary system are its familiarity and use of body-related units. An inch is about the size of a finger joint; a yard, the distance from the nose to the finger.

The Impact on Government and Education

Yet teachers find the customary system difficult to teach; students find it difficult to learn. Teachers and students alike find the metric system easier to deal with. They can handle 3.51 meters more easily than 3 yards, 2 feet, 6¼ inches. Teachers will spend less time teaching fractions and units of measurement. The American Association for the Advancement of Science found that slower children learn metric units faster than the customary units. The National Science Teacher's Association says that the metric system is easier for students to learn and use. So, after the changeover to metric, classes should be more pleasant than they are now.

7

Preparing for the Change

As a student prepares himself for his life's work, so the nation can prepare itself for the metric system. If a student waits until graduation to plan his career, he may find that he can't pursue his goals. Maybe he took the wrong subjects in high school, and can't enter college. Or maybe he lacks the tuition fee for a technical school. He may become discouraged and grab the first job that comes along. Later, he finds himself trapped in his dead-end job, possibly for life. Common sense and preparation could have made for a happier ending. So it will be for the nation in changing over to the metric system.

THINK METRIC

To prepare themselves, Americans must learn to *think metric*. To help, industry and government could conduct "Think Metric" campaigns. Industry can label their products now in both systems.

Why not start your own "Think Metric" campaign now? Just familiarize yourself with the common metric units. Use a metric ruler enough to learn the units of length. Measure the length of a desk, table, and bed in meters, and the lengths of your fingers in centimeters. Learn the kilogram and gram. Hold a kilogram of something in your hand to get the feel of it. Do the same with 500 and 250 grams.

When you have a few minutes, search the kitchen cabinet and supermarket shelves for packages, bottles, and cans whose contents are labeled in metric units. Try to guess the metric amount before you look at the label.

Estimate temperature in degrees Celsius, distance in kilometers, and speed in kilometers per hour. You won't do this very accurately, perhaps, but get as close as you can. Look over the table of comparisons in Chapter 3 and get the feel for each unit.

During Great Britain's transition period, the government aimed a "Think Metric" campaign at the citizens. They tried to convince the people to think in metric units rather than struggle with tedious conversions to customary. The government enlisted journalists and broadcasters in the campaign. Posters, exhibitions, local meetings, and study groups rounded out their efforts. After a couple of years, three out of four persons were familiar with the kilometer, and two out of three knew of the liter and kilogram.

In the United States, the mass media will emerge as the most important asset to a national "Think Metric" campaign. Most Americans will learn the metric units from television, radio, magazines, and newspapers. Industry and government will sponsor "Think Metric" advertisements. Some networks may air "Sesame Street"-type "Think Metric" programs. TV newscasters will use metric units in their reports.

Newspapers and magazines will include metric units in their stories. To ease their readers through the transition, they might introduce the units in steps. First, they will give measurements in customary units, followed by the metric equivalent in parentheses. For instance: "Mr. Jones swore that the spaceship was 30 feet (9 meters) tall." Later, they could reverse the order and give the metric units first. "Dr. Brown estimated the spaceship's height ap 15 meters (49 feet)." Finally, they will drop the customary units altogether. "The Mayor said that the spaceship was over 20 meters high."

When they give metric equivalents, most newspapers and magazines will round off. But some will need prodding. Years ago, a technical magazine started a "Think Metric" campaign. In each issue, they printed a picture of a beautiful girl and gave her measurements in both systems. A picture caption read, "Joan's measurements in inches are 37-24-37. In centimeters,

they are 93.98-60.96-93.96." Just as they had rounded off her measurements in customary units—her waist was unlikely to be exactly 24 inches around—so they should have rounded off the metric equivalents to read 94-61-94. After hundreds of prometric readers complained, they did just that.

Measurements in sports will change to metric units. This will help our athletes prepare better for international competitions, most of which now use metric units. The 100-meter dash, 200-meter swim, and 400-meter hurdles of the Olympics are examples. Some dimensions, such as the length of a football field, fall under the "rule of reason" and could remain untouched. But a change from yards to meters on the football field would give the "Think Metric" campaign a real boost. It would help prepare millions of football fans for the metric system.

PLAN NOW

The U.S. Metric Study found that few corporations and government agencies had yet thought much about the effects of the metric system. Worse, few intended to plan for the changeover. Most figured they would just sit back and wait for the federal government to lead the way.

A plan now will prevent disaster later. Suppose a company fails to study the effect of metric units when they purchase a new machine with an expected life of thirty years. In ten years, the market for customary-sized products may close. The company must scrap the machine, twenty years before it's due to wear out. If they had insisted that the machine be designed so they could convert it later to metric, they could have used it another twenty years.

In school, teachers could teach decimal fractions earlier than they do now, to prepare their students to handle the decimal relationships of the metric system. Teachers themselves must learn to use the metric system. The sooner they introduce it in their classes, the easier it will be for their students later. And the easier it will be for the nation, and for unborn generations to come.

Conversion Factors

TO CHANGE:	INTO:	MULTIPLY BY:
Acre	square meter	4,047
	hectare	.4047
Angstrom	meter	10^{-10}
	picometer	100
Astronomical Unit	gigameter	149.6
Atmosphere	kilopascal	101.3
Bar	kilopascal	100
Barn	square meter	10^{-28}
Barrel (petroleum 42 gallon)	liter	159
Bushel	cubic meter	.03524
	liter	35.24
Cable	meter	219.5
Caliber	millimeter	.254
Calorie (thermo-chemical)	joule	4.184
Carat (metric)	gram	.20
Celsius	kelvin	Add 273.15 to Celsius
Cord	cubic meter	3.625

YOU AND THE METRIC SYSTEM

TO CHANGE:	INTO:	MULTIPLY BY:
Cup	milliliter	236.6
Degree (angle)	centiradian	1.745
Dyne	micronewton	10
Erg	nanojoule	100
Fathom	meter	1.829
Foot	meter	.3048
	centimeter	30.48
Furlong	meter	201.2
Gallon (British)	liter	4.546
Gallon (U.S. dry)	liter	4.405
Gallon (U.S. liquid)	liter	3.785
Gill	centiliter	11.83
Grain	milligram	64.8
Hogshead	liter	238.5
Horsepower (electric)	watts	746
Hundredweight (long)	kilogram	50.8
Hundredweight (short)	kilogram	45.36
Inch	centimeter	2.54
Knot	kilometer per hour	1.852
Light year	terameter	9460
Micron	micrometer	1.0
Mil	micrometer	25.4
Mile (statute)	kilometer	1.609
Mile (nautical)	kilometer	1.852

Conversion Factors

TO CHANGE:	INTO:	MULTIPLY BY:
Minute (angle)	microradian	290.9
Ounce	gram	28.35
Ounce (fluid)	centiliter	2.957
Pace	meter	.762
Peck	liter	8.81
Pennyweight	gram	1.555
Pint (U.S. dry)	liter	.5506
	centiliter	55.06
Pint (U.S. liquid)	liter	.4732
	centiliter	47.32
Pound	kilogram	.4536
Quart (U.S. dry)	liter	1.101
Quart (U.S. liquid)	liter	.9464
	centiliter	94.64
Rod	meter	5.03
Second (angle)	microradian	4.848
Section	hectare	259
	square kilometer	2.59
Scruple	gram	1.296
Slug	kilogram	14.59
Tablespoon	milliliter	14.79
Teaspoon	milliliter	4.929
Ton (long)	metric ton	1.016
Ton (short)	metric ton	.9072
Yard	meter	.9144
	centimeter	91.44

Bibliography

Branley, Franklyn M. *Think Metric!* New York: Crowell, 1973

Deming, Richard. *Metric Power.* New York: Thomas Nelson, 1974

Donovan, Frank. *Let's Go Metric.* New York: Weybright, 1974

_____ . *Prepare Now for a Metric Future.* New York: Weybright, 1970

Hartsuch, Paul. *Think Metric Now!* Chicago: Follett, 1974

Hirsch, S. Carl. *Meter Means Measure.* New York: Viking, 1973

Kelley, Gerard W. *The Metric System Simplified.* New York: Sterling, 1973

Lamm, Joyce. *Let's Talk About the Metric System.* Middle village, N.Y.: Jonathan David, 1973

ASTM Standard Metric Practice Guide. Philadelphia, American Society for Testing and Materials, 1970

The following, available from the Superintendent of Documents, Washington, D.C., 20402, includes lists of publications by the National Bureau of Standards and the American National Standards Institute about conversion to the metric system:

Some references on metric information, with charts on all you need to know about metric and metric conversion factors. 1973. 11 p. (National Bureau of Standards, NBS special pub. 389) 25¢   S/N 0303-01219   C13.10:389

Index

Index